Listen to the Crows

The wily crow has long been celebrated in legend for his wisdom. Now Laurence Pringle explains the truth behind those legends. The crow is indeed one of the cleverest of creatures. Crows have learned to adapt to the changing world around them and to outwit the most watchful farmer.

Most important of all, crows have a language of their own—a way of warning or calling or greeting their fellows. One scientist has identified twenty-three different crow calls, and we know there are many more. Crows can count, and they seem to use this skill to identify themselves to others.

Listen carefully the next time you hear that familiar exchange of caws across a field. One crow may be telling another that a hawk is near, or announcing a feast of tender young corn seedlings. Or perhaps he is shouting out his name!

BY LAURENCE PRINGLE

ILLUSTRATED BY TED LEWIN

Listen to the Crows

Thomas Y. Crowell Company • New York

The author wishes to thank Dr. Nicholas S. Thompson,
Associate Professor of Psychology, Adjunct in Biology,
Clark University, for reading and suggesting
changes in the manuscript of this book.

BY THE AUTHOR:

Chains, Webs, and Pyramids: The Flow of Energy in Nature
Cockroaches: Here, There, and Everywhere
Follow a Fisher
Listen to the Crows
Twist, Wiggle, and Squirm: A Book About Earthworms
Water Plants

Copyright © 1976 by Laurence Pringle
Illustrations copyright © 1976 by Ted Lewin
All rights reserved. Except for use in a review,
the reproduction or utilization of this work in
any form or by any electronic, mechanical, or
other means, now known or hereafter invented,
including xerography, photocopying, and recording, and in any information storage and retrieval
system is forbidden without the written permission
of the publisher. Published simultaneously in
Canada by Fitzhenry & Whiteside Limited, Toronto.
Designed by Harriett Barton
Manufactured in the United States of America
Library of Congress Cataloging in Publication Data
Pringle, Laurence P
    Listen to the crows.
    Includes index. SUMMARY: Discusses the language
of the wary, clever crow. 1. Crows—Juv. lit. [1. Crows.
2. Animal communication] I. Lewin, Ted.
II. Title. QL696.P2367P74   598.8'64   75-43535
ISBN 0-690-01069-9 (CQR)

1   2   3   4   5   6   7   8   9   10

"If men had wings and bore black feathers,
few of them would be clever enough to be crows."

—HENRY WARD BEECHER

Caw . . . Caw . . . Caw!

A crow's voice, sharp and clear, cuts through the morning air. It is a bold and sassy sound.

Caw . . . Caw . . . Caw!

Most people pay no attention to this sound, or to the calls of other birds. But if you ask them about the loud, ringing call, they say, "Oh, that's a crow."

Almost everyone recognizes a few birds by sight: pigeons, gulls, robins. And crows. We know crows by their calls, by their large size (about twenty inches long), and by their glossy blackness. Crows are not plain black, though. If you get close to a crow, you will see glints of deep blue and purple on its feathers.

Caw . . . Caw . . . Caw . . . Caw . . . Caw! Listen to the crows. Sometimes they caw twice, sometimes several times. Have you ever wondered why?

1

SOME MEMBERS OF THE CROW FAMILY

SCRUB JAY

JACKDAW

RAVEN

ROOK

Very few people get close to crows. They are wary birds, and have learned that people are their worst enemies. But they are also clever birds. Crows are smart enough to find safe places even where millions of people live. You can see them in cities and suburbs, as well as in the country. They search for food along highways, just a few feet from speeding cars. They have learned that they are safe there, and that they can find all sorts of food, from popcorn to dead skunks.

Listen to the crows. Sometimes they caw slowly, sometimes fast and sharp. Sometimes they caw high, sometimes low. What do these different sounds mean?

The common crow lives in almost every state and far north into Canada. It also has close relatives in North America. The fish crow lives along the Atlantic coast and the Gulf of Mexico. It is smaller than the common crow, and says something like "car" instead of "caw." Far to the north lives another close relative, the common raven, a great, dark bird of rugged seacoasts and lonely mountaintops. It has a croaking call.

Worldwide, the crow family has about a hundred members, including jays, magpies, rooks, and jackdaws. Many scientists believe that the crow family is the most intelligent of all groups of birds. Crows are smarter than pigeons, gulls, and owls. On some kinds of tests, such as learning to seek food when a light is flashed, they do as well as rats and monkeys. A crow living on New Caledonia, an island in the Pacific Ocean, was observed using a tool. It held a slender twig in its beak and poked it into a hollow branch and underneath bark. The crow seemed to be trying to chase out insects to eat. Very few animals other than humans are known to use tools.

A NEW CALEDONIAN CROW WITH A TWIG "TOOL"

Listen to the crows. Some people have guessed at the meanings of crow sounds. A naturalist named Ernest Thompson Seton claimed that slow, unhurried caws mean, "All's well, come right along," and that a few quick caws mean, "Great danger—man with a gun!"

Crows show their intelligence by changing their ways whenever this helps them to survive. They adapt to new situations. One June evening in 1964, a biologist named Dwight R. Chamberlain was surprised to find more than 200 crows gathered in a Rochester, New York, cemetery. He was even more surprised at their behavior. The air was swarming with flying beetles, and the crows were after them. A crow would leave its perch, chase and catch a flying beetle, then return to its perch and eat the insect. Crows do not usually catch food on the wing, but there, in the fading light, they were doing it with the skill of fly-catchers.

4

CAW ... CAW ...CAW
"ALL'S WELL , COME RIGHT ALONG."

CAW! CAW! CAW! CAW! CAW!
"GREAT DANGER - MAN WITH A GUN!"

Crows eat just about anything—insects, earthworms, snails, clams, mice, fruit, grain, carrion (dead animals), and the eggs and young of other birds. About 650 different kinds of food have been found in the stomachs of crows. Their diet changes with the seasons. Beetles are abundant in May and June, so crows eat lots of beetles then. Later in the summer they fill up on the wild berries, crickets, and grasshoppers that are plentiful. Sometimes they raid vegetable gardens. A crow sometimes walks through a cornfield, pulling up the young plants to get at the sweet, tender, just-sprouted seeds. Delicious!

Some farmers try to kill crows or frighten them away. They once put up scarecrows to keep them away, but crows are not easily fooled. Some hunters also kill crows, for sport or because crows sometimes eat young ducks or other animals that hunters want for themselves. And so, in their efforts to outwit crows, farmers and hunters were among the first people who tried to understand the complex language of these birds.

Many birds have a language that is understood by others of the same kind. Male birds usually have a song which enables them to defend a territory. Its message is: "This is my home space. Keep away." The same song usually is also an advertisement for a mate. Birds make other sounds which mean, "Danger!" "Here is food," and, "Here I am" (a message to the other birds in a flock, or young in the nest).

How strange to think that the sweet melody of a robin is really tough talk, warning other male robins away! Somehow, the sounds that crows make seem much more like a language. Crows speak in rough, loud tones that resemble human voices. In fact, crows are excellent mimics of all sorts of sounds, including those made by people. Wild crows have been heard to mimic a crowing rooster, yelping puppy, barking dog, and meowing cat. Tame crows imitate human laughter, and can be taught to say, "Hello," "Goodbye," "Hot dog!" "Now you've done it!" and many other expressions, including a few which some people do not like to hear.

People once thought that a crow's tongue had to be split down the middle before the bird could "talk." This belief is not true. The idea probably started because crows have a small natural split at the tip of the tongue.

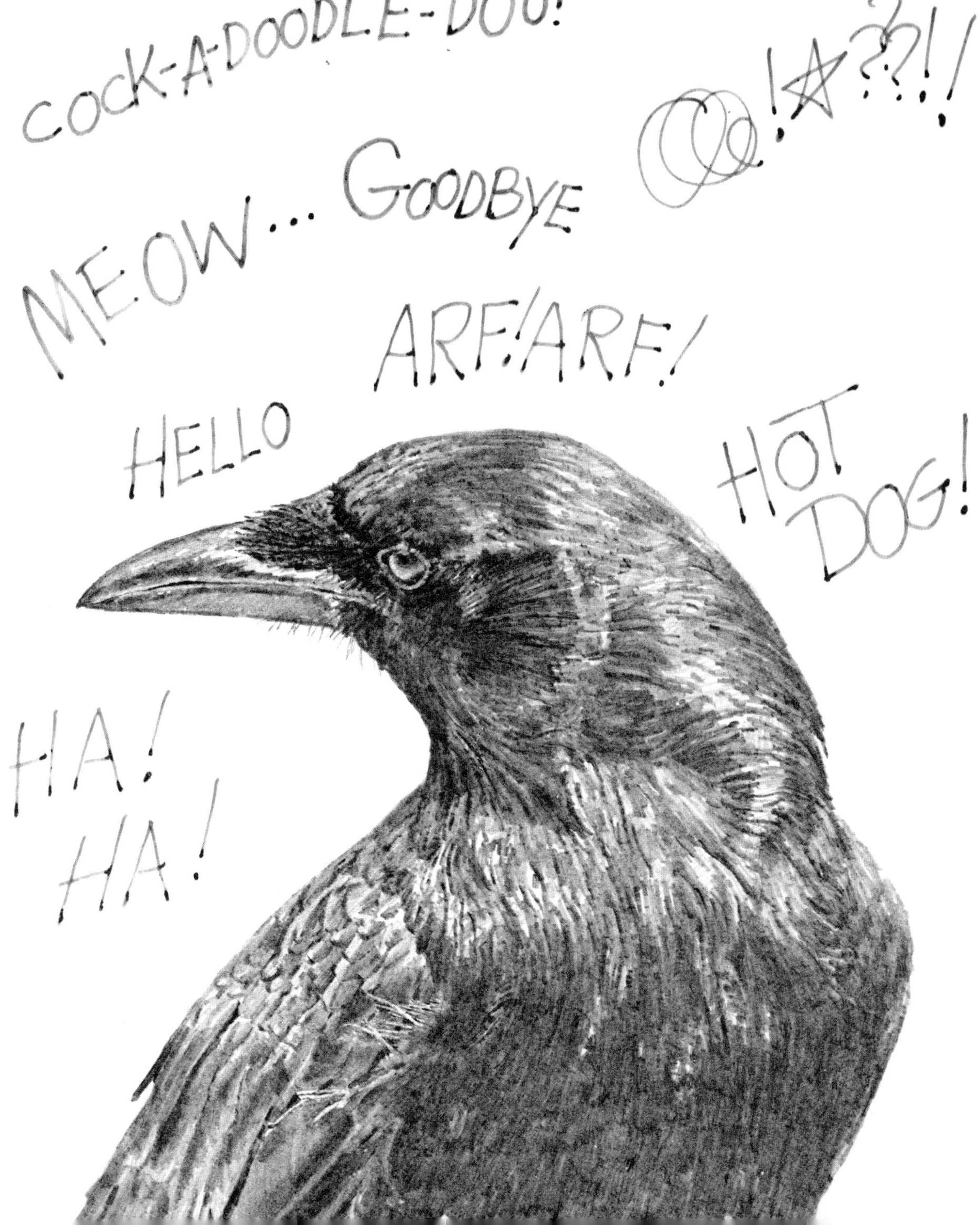
COCK-A-DOODLE-DOO!
MEOW... GOODBYE
ARF! ARF!
HELLO
HOT DOG!
HA! HA!

Listen to the crows. A small flock is flying over a group of pine trees. Suddenly one crow sees an owl hidden there. The crow wheels and dives, and calls: "Cawrr . . . Cawrr . . . Cawrr . . . Cawrr!" Its caws are stretched out, hoarse, and come quickly one right after another. This way of cawing has been named the "assembly" call. It has the sound of an emergency to it. Soon all the flock surrounds the owl, calling excitedly. Other crows rush to join in.

The assembly call is given when crows see or hear predators—animals which sometimes attack crows. Its message seems to be: "Help me drive off this enemy." Crow enemies include foxes, large hawks, and large owls. The great horned owl seems to be their worst enemy (other than people). It preys on crows year round, but especially in the wintertime, when crows gather by the thousands and sleep in groves of trees. Great horned owls swoop silently into these roosts and kill sleeping crows.

Whenever crows find a great horned owl or other enemy, they "mob" it. The assembly call rings out. All the crows within hearing distance may hurry to the source of the clamor. The air is filled with milling crows and their sounds.

Many crows perch near—but not *too* near—the owl. Some dart in to peck at it. If the owl flies, or just moves a bit on its branch, a great outcry goes up. The yelling chorus becomes an uproar. Mobbing may go on for hours, with some crows leaving to rest or feed, and others replacing them. If the owl finds a hiding place where the crows cannot reach it, the mob soon loses interest and all the crows leave. (Crows themselves are often chased and mobbed by blackbirds, kingbirds, or mockingbirds.

These birds are sometimes attracted to the sounds of crows mobbing an owl, and then mob some of the crows.)

Hunters learned about the assembly call long ago, and imitate it with their own voices or with calling devices made of wood or plastic. Some hunters now use recordings of crow voices. They broadcast the assembly call from a loudspeaker after concealing themselves in a special kind of hiding place called a blind. Often they set up an imitation or mounted great horned owl to fool the crows further.

Once a flock of crows is attracted by the assembly call, the boom of shotguns and the sight of dead crows may not be enough to stop the crows from mobbing a fake owl. The hunters keep giving the assembly call, and a falling dead crow looks like a *plunging* crow—a pattern of flight that excites other crows. Sooner or later, however, a crow becomes alarmed. It may catch a glimpse of a hidden hunter. It gives the "dispersal" call—short, sharp caws, close together. The birds quickly scatter.

Listen to the crows. A flock is feeding in a field, and a hunter is trying to sneak up on them. But two crows are perched in nearby trees, and they give the "alert" call, a few quick, sharp caws. The hunter creeps closer, and the crows give the dispersal call. As the hunter watches the flock fly off, he cannot help but admire the clever crows, which seem to post sentries so that the flock will not be surprised. But do crows really do this?

The scientists who study crow language doubt that crows ever say anything like: "You two stand guard while we have dinner." The so-called sentries may simply be members of the flock that are not hungry. Crows are wary birds, and nonfeeding crows would probably rest in trees or other high perches

rather than on the ground. This may explain why crows appear to have sentries.

Besides, the so-called sentries are not always effective. Four different times when biologist Dwight R. Chamberlain approached a flock of feeding crows, the "sentry" flew off without making a sound. The flock was still on the ground, and was surprised, when Chamberlain came into sight.

Dwight Chamberlain has studied crows and their language for several years. He examined the syrinx, or "voice box," of crows and found that it has six pairs of muscles—only one pair less than most songbirds have. Ducks, hawks, and many other kinds of birds have only two or three pairs of muscles in their syrinx. A crow's voice box is well designed to produce a great variety of sounds.

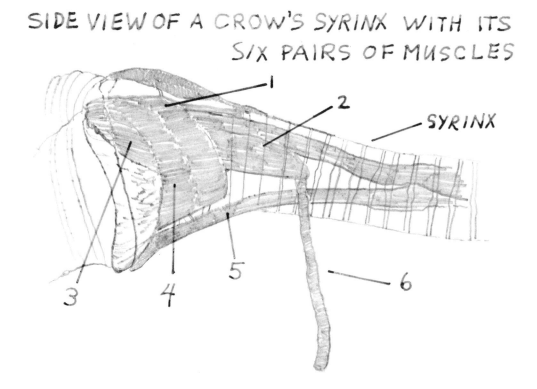

SIDE VIEW OF A CROW'S SYRINX WITH ITS
SIX PAIRS OF MUSCLES

Since the early 1900s, scientists like Dwight Chamberlain have tried to figure out the messages that crows send to each other. During the 1960s it became possible to make clear tape recordings of wild animal sounds, and Chamberlain has recorded the calls of hundreds of crows, both wild and tame. Sometimes he used live great horned owls in order to attract a mob of crows and record their sounds. A special sound-gathering device was used to record distant crow calls. (The same kind of equipment is used to record a quarterback's signals during telecasts of football games.)

Dwight Chamberlain gave names to most of the different kinds of calls he recorded. Some of these calls, such as assembly and dispersal, had been recognized before. But Chamberlain named many more. For example, he divided the mobbing calls of crows into three kinds—assembly, scolding, and modified scolding. The last two kinds of calls, he found, are given when a crow hears an unseen owl or other predator, and also when a crow sees a predator in the distance. Once a crow is close to the predator, it gives the assembly call. Crows also give these three calls when they hear the wailing "squalling" cry of a crow that is struggling to escape from a predator. They have been heard to growl, too, as they dive close to a predator.

Chamberlain taped other calls of crows in their winter roosts at night. One was a strange "wah-oo" sound he heard several times just after sunset. The most common sounds in the roosts, however, were "threat" calls, usually given when two crows wanted to perch in the same place. To settle these disputes they use a great variety of sounds, including screams, cackles, coos, rattles, and growls.

Rattling sounds are also given by a male crow when he courts a female. He faces her, puffs out his feathers, and bows low. The rattling song begins when his head is high and ends at the bottom of his bow. It may be repeated as many as fifty times. Pairs of crows, and groups of young, also rattle as they dive and tumble in the air.

Twenty-three different calls were recorded and described by Chamberlain, and these are not all the sounds that crows make. One unusual sound he recorded was a soft "contentment" note

SCREAM CACKLE

COO RATTLE

GROWL

made by tame crows when their throats were gently stroked. No one knows whether wild crows make this sound.

Dwight Chamberlain broadcast to wild crows many of the recordings he made. As you might expect, crows usually flew toward him when he played the scolding, squalling, or assembly calls. They usually fled when they heard a recording of the dispersal call. But they often did not respond at all to several other calls. The language of crows still holds many mysteries.

Listen to the crows. Three baby crows are in their nest, high in a tree. It is a big, sturdy nest, made of sticks and lined with softer materials such as grasses, moss, and deer hair. The little

crows are hungry. They give hoarse little caws. Then a parent flies into sight, and a great chorus of high-pitched cries comes from the young crows. The clamor reaches a peak as the parent lands. Then food is stuffed into each gaping red mouth, and each nestling gives a little, gulping yip as it is fed.

After listening to the sounds made by hungry young crows, can you really say that there is just one feeding call? This question has been raised by Nicholas S. Thompson, a psychology professor who teaches at Clark University in Worcester, Massachusetts. He has studied crow language for about ten years, first in Pennsylvania, then in Massachusetts. He disagrees with the idea that crows have a certain set of calls that, like highway signs, are always used in a specific situation and that always produce a specific action in other crows. This may be true of other kinds of birds, but Thompson believes that crow language is more complicated.

Some crow calls do seem like highway signs. There is no doubt about the meaning of the assembly call—to crows, hunters, scientists, and perhaps owls too. Nicholas Thompson believes, however, that many crow calls that have been given labels are really part of a series that expresses different degrees of feeling in crows. For example, the so-called "feeding" sound of young crows is not always the same. The calls of nestlings get louder and more rapid as their food is brought closer. Their calls also vary with their hunger—the nestlings that have not been fed for a long time seem to make more noise than those which have been recently fed.

I AM SORT OF ANGRY

I AM ANGRY

CAW CAW CAWCAW

Nicholas Thompson believes that "the closer a crow is to some urgent or important situation, the more intense, the more rapid, the more variable, and the more drawn out become its caws."

And so, the sound that has been named a crow's feeding call really varies a lot. The sounds of crows also change in other situations. In mobbing, for instance, a crow's calls change as it nears a mob, joins the mob, and gets close to the owl or other predator which is the center of attention. Instead of dividing mobbing calls into three types, Nicholas Thompson suggests that all the calls are part of an unbroken series that expresses a crow's growing excitement. At a distance from the mob, a crow's message may be: "I am sort of angry." Then, within a few moments, its message changes to: "I am angry," then: "I am very angry!" and finally: "I am very, *very* angry!"

Listen to the crows. Several of them sit in a tree, watching a group of hunters cross a distant field. The hunters are far away, so the alert signal is not given. Instead the crows caw as though

20

I AM VERY, VERY ANGRY!

I AM VERY ANGRY!

CAWCAW CAWCAW

they were chatting with one another. Some people observing this scene would say that the crows are counting the hunters.

Most kinds of birds cannot count. Nature photographers sometimes take advantage of this fact when they set up a blind near a bird nest. Two people enter the blind, then one leaves. So far as the bird is concerned, "People came, people left; now I can relax." It is less fearful of the blind, and the photographer inside has a better chance of getting good pictures.

Hunters have tried the same trick on crows, and report that it does not work. Some people claim that crows can count up to six. Humorist Ed Zern once described a plan for outwitting such crows. It involved twenty-five hunters, all dressed alike and about the same size, dashing back and forth in groups of different numbers between a barn and a blind. Some of the men would wear false mustaches, which they would exchange with others from time to time. According to the plan, after several minutes

1 2 3 4 5 6
1 2 3 4 5 6
3 4 5 6

of back-and-forth running, the goal would be achieved: the watching crows would have lost count; all the men would seem to have departed, but there would be one hunter left in the blind.

Crows can count. Their counting ability has been shown by tests with captive crows. No proof has been found that they count in all the ways that people do—or that they count hunters. The crow's ability to count probably developed millions of years ago, perhaps even before humans lived on earth. Scientists believe that the ability developed because it helps crows survive in their day-to-day life. But how?

A psychologist named David G. Nichols suggested that crows use their counting ability in their plain, everyday cawing—their most common sound—and that this enables individual crows to identify themselves to others. In 1966, Nicholas Thompson decided to investigate this idea.

With help from his family and from college students, Thompson recorded and analyzed the caws of dozens of wild crows. He found that the crows caw in "bursts," or sets, of one to nine caws. But bursts of more than seven caws were rarely used. Most of the crows made bursts of one to six caws. The caws themselves differed—some crows made longer caws than others did. And the time between caws also differed—some crows paused for a longer time between caws.

From this information, Thompson decided that David G. Nichols' idea was correct. Crows can tell each other apart by their caws. Each crow in a flock gives itself a sort of name—by using different numbers of caws in a burst, long or short caws, and long or short pauses between the caws.

Crow A might give bursts usually made up of three long caws. Crow B might also give bursts of three caws, but the caws would be longer than those by Crow A. Crow C might give bursts of five caws. Crow D might also give this number of caws, but with longer pauses between the caws in each burst. And so on.

The message each crow gives is simple. One says, "I am a crow." When a second crow gives its special pattern of caws, it says, "I am another crow." And a third crow says, "I am another crow different from the other two."

These simple messages are valuable to crows because they travel and search for food in loose flocks. Often crows cannot see other members of their flock. Just by listening, though, they can keep track of them, and of their own location within a widely scattered and moving flock. A crow can quickly "tell" the others about food or a predator it finds.

Suppose a crow is in the center of its flock, and lands to eat a few grasshoppers. The rest of the flock keeps flying, but the feeding crow calls, and the rest of the flock knows where it is. After eating, the crow takes to the air again, but it does not get confused or lost. By listening to the other crows, it can figure out its location with respect to the flock—perhaps now on the fringe of the flock's left side.

A crow does not give its special cawing pattern perfectly every time, but it does not usually miss by much. If its special pattern is three caws, it gives mostly threes, along with some bursts of twos and fours.

No one knows how long a crow keeps its special pattern of cawing. The pattern is like a name, but a crow does not have to keep the same name forever. A crow can change its cawing pattern frequently; Thompson heard one crow run through five or six patterns in a few minutes. Perhaps each crow has a few favorite cawing patterns that it uses throughout life. It may change to another pattern when other crows with similar pat-

CAW.. CAW .. CAW .. CAW

CAW!
CAW!

terns come within hearing. The important thing, for the good of the flock, is that every individual should have a distinct pattern at any one time.

Nicholas Thompson continues to investigate the language of crows, recording more crow calls and studying them. Besides the usual calls, he has recorded an unusual series of sounds that seem to come from young wild crows in the summer and early fall, as they grow into adults. The sounds remind him of the babbling of babies. In just a few moments, and in no apparent order, the crow gives high and low notes, fast and slow notes—just about every sound a crow can make. Thompson wonders if he was listening to a young crow running through the "ABCs" of its language, as a young child might.

Listen to the crows. Spring is here, and rattling calls can be heard as a pair of crows nest in a grove of trees near a house. A hunter lives in the house, but he does not bother the crows. Since 1973 a federal law has protected crows from hunters in every state for most of the year, especially during the time when they raise their young. Besides, the hunter is fond of crows. He likes to have them around.

People used to argue about crows. Some people said that crows were bad because they ate corn and raided the nests of ducks and songbirds. Other people said that crows were good because they ate lots of insect pests. Now our ideas about crows, and all of nature, are changing. To think that any living thing is all good or all bad is silly. Crows are just crows. They are part of nature, and everything in nature, one way or another, is valuable.

We still have much to learn about the language of crows. They have a lot to say. Their sounds and their intelligence may help us to understand the language of other animals, including humans. They are out there now, cawing back and forth—rattling, cooing, mimicking. What are they saying to each other?

Perhaps you can help solve this puzzle. To begin, just listen to the crows.

Index

About the Author

Laurence Pringle is the author of twenty books, whose subjects range from dinosaurs and their world to environmental problems today. His concern with nature and ecology has led him to supplement scholarly research with firsthand investigation. Mr. Pringle, who has degrees in wildlife conservation from Cornell University and the University of Massachusetts, is a gifted photographer, illustrating many of his books with his own photographs. He shares an acre of land in West Nyack, New York, with katydids, woodchucks, garter snakes, screech owls, wildflowers, and—of course—crows.

About the Artist

The illustrations for LISTEN TO THE CROWS reflect Ted Lewin's continuing interest in ecology and conservation. He has toured the East African game reserves, backpacked in the Haleakala Crater on Maui, and gone whale-watching off the coast of Baja California. Born in Buffalo and educated at the Pratt Institute of Art in Brooklyn, Mr. Lewin is the illustrator of many children's books and magazine articles. He has recently written and illustrated a book on the Florida Everglades, which he and his wife, Betsy, explore by canoe every year.